Smoothie

Tasty shakes and blends.

A collection of delicious, healthy smoothie recipes for all the family!

(im)PulsePaperbacks

Smoothie basics

A smoothie is a delicious and nutritious drink made up of blended fruit and or vegetables. Traditionally, smoothies are considered healthy drinks as the basic ingredients are typically packed with the vitamins and nutrients needed to maintain a healthy balanced diet, and in their most basic form they are an excellent way of ensuring that we eat lots of fruit and vegetables. They are also a great way of making sure that kids receive essential nutrients, as many smoothies look pretty yummy when made - not unlike milkshakes!

By creating your own smoothies, you may have to invest a little time, but you will in the long term save yourself money - even if you have to buy equipment to begin with. And for those times when you fancy something that is naughty as well as nice we have included a few indulgent recipes - and even a few that contain alcohol (these are clearly marked).

To grab a smoothie on the go, make them up ahead of time. You can freeze a smoothie and thaw it out when you want it but remember that you'll need to allow some space in the container because your smoothie will likely expand when freezing.

The only equipment that you really need to make a smoothie is a blender. Smoothie making is very simple, but here are some tips and ideas to keep in mind.

The first step in making a smoothie is assembling your ingredients and there are four different categories of ingredients that you can use.

Liquids

These help to give your smoothie a thinner, drinkable consistency. Add the liquids to the blender first, to prevent it from binding up on the frozen fruit and getting stuck.

Fruit Juice

Any fruit juice works great; try squeezing the juice of an orange or lemon for a fresh flavour.

Milk

Using skimmed milk or soy milk adds protein and a creamy flavour and is also a healthier option than full fat milk.

Water

Plain water is sometimes the best option, especially if you have a lot of flavours going on with the other ingredients.

Solid ingredients

These often make up the bulk of your smoothie, and for this category you will often have more than one of the following:

Yoghurt
Plain yoghurt is ideal if you are adding in your own fruit, since the fruit-infused yoghurts have hidden added sugars.

Fresh Fruits
Any fresh fruit — peaches, pears, mangos, and more — can be added to a smoothie; just remove any seeds and skin and toss into the blender. (See back of book for nutritional value of fruits).

Tofu
A smoothie with tofu will have added protein, which is important especially if you are drinking the smoothie for a meal; choose the silken kind as it is much creamier than the firm varieties.

Peanut Butter
This will add healthful fats and protein and great flavour, especially delicious with bananas.

Fruits or vegetables

The recipes don't always specify, but if you have time to freeze your fruit beforehand, your smoothie will stay colder and be thicker than if your fruit is warm.

Large fruits (like bananas or melons) should be chopped into pieces before freezing. Spread the pieces on a plate or baking sheet while in the freezer which will make sure the fruit doesn't freeze in one big unmanageable lump. Once frozen, then you can store them together in a freezer bag or container. Using frozen strawberries, blueberries, or even mixed berries will add a sweet and slightly tart flavour.

Flavour Add-ins

These can pull all the flavours in the smoothie together and provide a "kick"; as an added bonus, the following also add a nutritional punch:

Cinnamon
Any spice, particularly cinnamon, can add flavour as well as boost the nutritional properties of your smoothie.

Ginger
Either freshly grated or powdered ginger will add a great spicy flavour to the smoothie.

Mint
Fresh herbs such as mint or parsley give smoothies a fresh flavour. Just give a rough chop before tossing into the blender.

Berry Berry Smoothie/Serves 2

2 kiwis, peeled and cut into 4 pieces
1 banana
5 strawberries
7 raspberries
335g/1 1/2 cup low fat natural yoghurt
1 medium size glass milk

Directions

Put all ingredients in the blender, blend until desired consistency, serve immediately.If you think it is too thick, just add more milk.

Berry Bomb Smoothie/Serves 2

20 blueberries
20 strawberries
2 mangos
25ml/3 tsps pure apple juice

Directions

Cut the mangos up into small pieces then add to blender. Next add the apple juice, blueberries and strawberries. Blend until smooth. For a more creamier and colder version, try adding a little bit of vanilla ice cream to the mix.

Berry Burst Smoothie/Serves 2

1 handful of raspberries
1 chopped mango
1 lime (juice only)
2 peeled oranges
splash of apple juice
6 ice cubes

Directions

Blend together your mango, oranges and raspberries. Then add your lime juice and splash of apple juice, blend again. Finally add your ice, blend until cubes are crushed.

Berry Delight/Serves 2

150ml/2/3 cup raspberry yoghurt
75ml/1/3 cup natural yoghurt
50ml/3 tbsps milk
50g/1/2 cup frozen raspberries
2 pears peeled, cored and chopped

Directions

Blend all ingredients for 30 seconds until smooth, keeping a little of the natural yoghurt aside to dribble on top of your finished smoothie.

Berry Refresher/Serves 2

2 bananas
115g/1 cup of raspberries
60g/1/2 cup frozen blueberries
10-12 frozen strawberries
225-450ml/1-2 cups cranberry juice

Directions

Place all ingredients in a blender and blend until smooth.

Berry-Tastic Smoothie/Serves 2

1 handful of blueberries
3 plums
1/2 glass of cranberry juice
60ml/4 tbsps of Greek yoghurt
1 banana
4-5 ice cubes

Directions

Remove the stone from the plums and roughly chop them and place in the blender. Add the blueberries, banana, cranberry juice, greek yoghurt, then the ice.

Berry Tropical Fruit Smoothie/Serves 4

2 apples
6 large strawberries
1 large cup of berries
1 large cup of chopped/cubed pineapple
1 medium cup of ice (cubed or crushed)
1 medium cup of fresh orange juice
1 pot of natural yoghurt

Directions

Put everything in the blender and blast on the highest speed. The ice makes it cold and the yoghurt adds flavour and makes it creamy.

Blackberry Icecream Smoothie/Serves 2

60g/1/2 cup blackberries (fresh or frozen)
110ml/1/2 cup vanilla ice cream
1/2 banana
110ml/1/2 cup milk

Directions

Blend the milk with the banana and and blackberries until a slushy texture is formed. Add ice cream for extra sweetness and blend till smooth.

Blissful Berry Smoothie/Serves 2

115g/1 medium cup of raspberries
115g/1 medium cup of strawberries
1 banana
450ml/2 cups of orange juice

Directions

Put all the fruit and juice into the blender, then blend until smooth.

Blackberry & Cherry / Serves 2

115g/1 cup cherries
60g/1/2 cup of blackberries
1 large glass of water

Directions

Place ingredients in the blender and blend until smooth.

Blackberry & Melon / Serves 2

300g/2 cups of frozen blackberries
340g/2 cups honeydew melon (fresh or frozen)
70g/1/3 cup of sugar (or more to taste)

Directions

Place ingredients in the blender and blend until smooth.

Blueberry Blast / Serves 2

110ml/1/2 cup of skimmed milk
120g/1 cup of low fat vanilla ice cream
300g/2 cups of frozen blueberries

Directions

Place ingredients in the blender and blend until smooth.

Blackcurrant Blast / Serves 2

230g/2 cups fresh blackcurrants
150g/1 cup blueberries
1 tsp of honey or sugar (optional)

Directions

Place ingredients in the blender and blend until smooth.

Cheery Cherry/Serves 2

approx 20 cherries
1 apple
1 banana
1 kiwi
1 handful of blueberries
cloudy apple juice

Directions

Stone the cherries and put into the blender. Add the chopped apple, banana, kiwi and blueberries. Blend with a splash of apple juice to loosen.

Cherry Apple Pie/Serves 2

1/2 cup of frozen mixed berries
1/2 ltr/2 1/4 cups apple juice
2 tbsps of honey
1 tbsp of natural yoghurt

Directions

Add mixed berries to blender, then add apple juice, honey and yoghurt. Blend until smooth. Serve and enjoy.

Cinnamon Surprise/Serves 2

2 bananas
1 small cup of frozen raspberries
1 small cup of frozen blueberries
1 small cup of pure orange juice
1 tsp vanilla essence
1 tsp maple syrup
3 ice cubes
cinnamon to taste

Directions

Place all ingredients in the blender and blend until smooth. The more cinnamon added the more delicious it is.

Raspberry & Lemon Smoothie/Serves 1

15 raspberries
lemonade - a good splash (should not cover the raspberries)

Directions

Place raspberries in the blender, pour over some lemonade (making sure you don't cover them). Blend for approximately 20 seconds, serve and enjoy.

Raspberry & Orange Tang Smoothie/Serves 2

10 raspberries
juice squeezed from 5 oranges
50ml/1 2/3fl oz still water
50ml/1 2/3fl oz cranberry juice

Directions

Place raspberries in the blender first, then add the freshly squeezed orange juice. Blend for 10-15 seconds. Add cranberry juice and water. Mix on high for 8 more seconds.

Tip: This smoothie has more of a juice consistency than being a thick smoothie consistency, so if you prefer it to be thicker just add less or no water.

Raspberry Ripple Smoothie/Serves 2

1 medium banana
75g/1/2 cup of red raspberries (or strawberries)
75g/1/2 cup of blackberries (or blueberries)
110ml/1/2 cup of yoghurt
110ml/1/2 cup of ice

Directions

Cut the raspberries into small pieces that will fit through a straw. Blend the banana, ice, and yoghurt with the blackberries. Layer alternating chopped raspberries and smoothies through the glass.

Banana Smoothie/Serves 4

55ml/1/4 cup orange juice
4 bananas
3 scoops of plain ice cream
2 tbsps of golden syrup
3 tbsps of plain yoghurt
lemon juice (optional)
sugar (optional)

Directions

Cut the bananas into small pieces and put in the blender. Add all the other ingredients. Blend on full for 20 seconds. Put lemon juice around the rim of the glasses then roll the rim in the sugar so it sticks to the lemon juice.

Banana Apple Smoothie/Serves 1

1 whole banana, chopped into 4 pieces
1 whole apple, peeled and chopped into 4 pieces
110ml/1/2 cup of pure orange juice
55ml/1/4 cup low fat milk

Directions

Place all ingredients in the blender for approximately 20 seconds.

Banana Berry Smoothie/Serves

1 banana
110g/1/2 cup of low fat vanilla yoghurt
60g/1/2 cup of frozen peaches
115g/1 cup of frozen strawberries
1 tbsp of orange juice concentrate

Directions

Roughly chop the banana, then place all ingredients in the blender, (add ice if preferred to fill blender), blend until smooth.

Banana Delight Smoothie/Serves 2

2 bananas
1 tbsp of Greek yoghurt
1 large tsp of Nutella
1 handful of crushed ice
275ml/1/2 pint of milk

Directions

Chop bananas then add them and all remaining ingredients to the blender. Blend, pour and enjoy. You can always add more Nutella to taste.

Banana Mania Smoothie/Serves 1

2 bananas
6 strawberries
5 raspberries
1 clementine

Directions

Blend the fruits together first, then gradually add 2 ice cubes and blend until smooth.

Banana Peach Smoothie/Serves 1

1 small banana, or half a large banana
100g/1/2 cup unsweetened canned peaches, drained
225ml/1 cup milk

Directions

Blend all ingredients together with 110ml/1/2 cup of ice cubes until smooth.

Banana Cherry Smoothie/Serves 2

1 banana, chopped into 4
130g/1 cup of sweet cherries (pitted and stem removed)
juice from 1/2 lemon
110ml/1/2 cup of low-fat plain yoghurt
5 cubes of ice
2 drops of almond extract (optional)

Directions

Put all ingredients in the blender and blend until smooth. Should you require a hint of almond, then add the drops of almond extract.

Banana Blackberry Smoothie/Serves 2

2 chopped bananas
200ml/7/8 cup milk
200g/3/4 cup Greek yoghurt, chilled
1 tbsp clear honey
300g/2 cups fresh blackberries
Extra banana, yoghurt and blackberries to serve, optional

Directions

Blend all of the ingredients together for approximately 20 seconds. Place a spoonful of yoghurt in the base of 2 serving glasses and add a few blackberries and slices of banana then add the smoothie and serve.

Banana Honey Smoothie/Serves 2

1 medium sized banana
honey flavoured yoghurt (add according to taste)
2 tsps honey
1/2 mug of milk

Directions

Place all ingredients into a blender (leave a couple of slices of banana for later). Mix for 10 seconds at low speed, then mix again for 5 seconds at high speed. Serve into glasses and put the banana slices which you left to one side on the rim of each glass. Serve, drink and enjoy.

Strawberry & Pineapple Smoothie/Serves 1

300g/2 cups of chilled fresh or frozen strawberries, slightly thawed
225ml/1 cup of chilled pineapple or orange juice
225g/8oz carton of low-fat vanilla yoghurt
1 tbsp of sugar

Directions

In a blender, combine all ingredients. Cover and blend for between 1-2 minutes until nearly smooth.

Strawberry Yoghurt Smoothie/Serves 1

half ripe mango
6 fresh/frozen strawberries
1 banana
1 small apple
5 tbsps strawberry yoghurt
5 ice cubes

Directions

Peel and chunk all the fruit and put in blender, add yoghurt then ice cubes. Blend for approx 40 seconds till smooth.

Strawberry Cherry Berry Smoothie/Serves 4

450g/3 cups frozen pitted dark sweet cherries
450g/3 cups frozen whole strawberries
675ml/3 cups cranberry juice

Directions

In a blender, puree half the frozen pitted dark sweet cherries, half the frozen strawberries and half the cranberry juice, stirring as needed, until smooth. Pour into two serving glasses.

Repeat with remaining ingredients for two more servings.

Simply Strawberry/Serves 2

12 strawberries
200g of strawberry yoghurt
1 scoop of strawberry icecream

Directions

Chop the strawberries and blend with yoghurt and icecream. Serve and garnish with strawberry pieces..

Strawberry De-lish/Serves 2

Half a punnet of strawberries
1 large ripe mango
1 banana

Directions

Place ingredients in the blender and blend until smooth.

Strawberry Fizz/Serves 2

250g/1 2/3 cups of strawberries
2 apples, cored and chopped into large cubes
300ml orange juice

Directions

Put all ingredients into the blender, and blend until desired consistency.

Strawberry Burst /Serves 1

2 bananas
1 orange
2 kiwis
10-12 frozen strawberries
1/2 cup of frozen blueberries
1-2 cups of orange juice

Directions

Blend all ingredients together and serve chilled.

Strawberry Sweetie/Serves 2

6 large strawberries
1 oz/2 tbsps strawberry syrup
2 oz/4 tbsps milk

Directions

Place the strawberries in blender, then add the ice, syrup then the milk.

Smooth Strawberries /Serves 2

2 bananas
10-12 frozen strawberries
1 cup of apple juice

Directions

Blend all ingredients together and serve chilled.

Strawberry Apple/Serves 2

150g/1 cup of strawberries
1 apple

Directions

Cut up the strawberries and the apple, placein blender and blend until desired consistency.

Strawberry & Mango/Serves 2

2 handfuls of strawberries (sliced and hulled)
1 large mango (sliced)
1 1/2 medium size cups of pure orange juice
4 ice cubes

Directions

Place all ingredients into a blender, blend until there are no lumps. Put mixture in the fridge for 5-10 minutes, then serve, drink immediately and enjoy.

Pineapple & Melon Slush Smoothie/Serves 2

110ml/1/2 cup of pineapple juice
4 tbsps orange juice
125g/2/3 cup of galia melon
140g/2/3 cup of pineapple chunks
4 crushed ice cubes

Directions

Pour the orange and pineapple juice into a food processor and blend together gently until combined. Add the melon, pineapple chunks and ice and blend until it reaches a slushy consistency. Pour into glasses and decorate with slice of orange or pineapple. Serve at once.

Passion Fruit, Pineapple and Mango Smoothie/Serves 1

2 passion fruits, pulp only
1 small mango, cut into chunks
75g/1/2 cup pineapple, cut into chunks
75ml/1/3 cup of pineapple juice
1 lime, juice only
7 ice cubes
a pinch of ground black pepper
a pinch of cayenne pepper (optional)

Directions

Blend all of the ingredients together until smooth. If you prefer your smoothie to have a little "kick" add a pinch of cayenne pepper.

Pineapple & Coconut Smoothie/Serves 2

250g/1 2/3 cups of cubed/chopped pineapple
1 scoop vanilla ice-cream
1/3 small cup of coconut
1 banana
2 medium cups of milk
2 ice cubes

Directions

Add all ingredients to the blender. Blend for approximately 30 seconds or until desired consistency. Serve and enjoy immediately.

Pineapple Crush Smoothie/Serves 1

110ml/1/2 cup pineapple juice
4 tbsps orange juice
150g/3/4 cup melon, roughly chopped
1 cup frozen pineapple chunks
4 ice cubes

Directions

Pour the pineapple juice and orange juice into a blender and process gently until combined. Add the melon, pineapple, and ice cubes and process until slushy. Pour into glasses.

Papaya & Honey Smoothie/Serves 1

1 large papaya
2 tbsps honey
Cinnamon to taste
200ml/2/3 cup of greek style yoghurt
Handful of ice

Directions

De-stone and de-skin papaya, chop into chunks and blend all ingredients until smooth.

Apple & Pear Smoothie/Serves 2

1 tbsp mixed seeds (sesame, sunflower, or flaxseed)
1 small apple
1 small ripe pear
3/4 cup of milk
Vanilla extract (few drops)

Directions

Blend all ingredients together for about 30 seconds or until you have reached the required consistency. If the smoothie is too thick add additional liquids to taste.

Apple & Carrot Smoothie/Serves 1

1 apple, large, sweet
1 banana, large, ripe
1 carrot, large
1 orange, large
3 dates, pitted
1 tbsp flax seed, whole, raw
1 cup ice cubes

Directions

Blend together the apple, banana, carrot and orange. Add the dates, flax seed and the ice. Cover the blender and blend at high speed until smooth.

Mango & Ginger/Serves 4

245g/8oz low fat vanilla yoghurt
225ml/1 cup of non-fat buttermilk
2 pieces of crystallized ginger (approx. 1 oz)
2 ripe mangos, peeled and chopped into small pieces
110ml/1/2 cup of crushed ice

Directions

In the blender purée the fruit and ginger, scraping down the sides as necessary. Add the buttermilk, yoghurt and ice and purée until smooth and frothy. Add crushed ice. Serve chilled.

Mango & Pineapple Breeze/Serves 2

340ml/12fl oz can of frozen orange juice concentrate
170ml/6fl oz of mango premium nectar
225ml/1 cup of pineapple juice
225ml/1 cup of ice cubes

Directions

Place all ingredients into blender, and process until smooth.

Mango Madness/Serves 2

450g/2 cups of low-fat vanilla yoghurt
225ml/1 cup mango nectar
2 mangos, peeled and chopped
1/4 tsp of cardamom

Directions

Place all ingredients into blender, and process until smooth

Peachy Berry Smoothie/Serves 2

1/2 cup ripe medium peaches, diced
1/2 cup raspberries
1/2 cup peach nectar
1 cup low-fat peach yoghurt

Directions

Combine the yoghurt and nectar in a blender. Add the raspberries and peaches. Blend until smooth.

Peachy Orange Smoothie/Serves 2

1/2 tin of peaches
2 tbsps of natural yoghurt
250-400ml/1-2 cups of fresh orange juice

Directions

Open the tin of peaches and put half of the peaches into the blender (pour approx two thirds of the syrup in also). Next, add the natural yoghurt. Finally add between 250-400ml/1-2 cups of the orange juice depending on preference. Blend well, serve and enjoy.

Peach & Apple Smoothie/Serves 1

1 small apple
100g/1/2 cup peach halves (from a can) chopped
Syrup from can of peach halves
200g/2/3 cup natural yoghurt
3 ice-cubes
1/2 tsp vanilla essence
Small pinch of sugar
2 tbsps honey

Directions

Place all ingredients in the blender, then blend for approximately 25 seconds or until smooth.

Tropical Kiwi Smoothie/Serves 2

2 kiwi fruits
2 bananas, sliced
8 strawberries, topped and cut in half
1 pear
10 fl oz/1/2 pint of fresh blackcurrant juice

Directions

Peel and de-core the pear and peel and slice the kiwi. Put all fruit including the fresh blackcurrant juice into a blender then blend for approximately 30 seconds until smooth and thick. Serve and enjoy.

Kiwi Tang Smoothie/Serves 2

75g/1/2 cup of fresh diced kiwi
75g/1/2 cup of lime sherbet
150g/1 cup of diced ripe banana
170g/1 cup of diced honeydew melon

Directions

Put all ingredients in the blender then blend until smooth.

Kiwi Dream Smoothie/Serves 1

150ml/2/3 cup milk
juice of 2 limes
2 kiwi fruit, peeled and chopped
1 tbsp sugar
450ml/2 cups vanilla ice cream

Directions

Add the milk, lime juice, sugar and ice cream and blend until mixed and smooth. Then add the kiwi fruit and process until smooth. .

Kiwi Burst/Serves 2

2 peeled kiwi fruits
55g/1/2 cup of diced honeydew melon
110ml/1/2 cup of low fat lemon yoghurt
150g/1 cup frozen green grapes
1 tbsp of chopped fresh mint
fresh lemon juice to taste (if preferred)

Directions

Put the kiwi, honeydew melon and lemon yoghurt in a blender. Next add the grapes and mint then blend until smooth. Taste and add lemon juice if you like.

Kiwi Kiss Smoothie/Serves 2

2 kiwi's
12 strawberries
1 banana
1 tbsp of honey
4 large ice cubes

Directions

Slice bananas into four. Cut tops off strawberries, peel and dice kiwi's, add all to blender. Add 1 tablespoon of honey then 4 ice cubes and blend for approx. 20 seconds.

Green Fruit Smoothie/Serves 2

2 peeled kiwi fruits
approx 25 frozen green grapes, halved
1 frozen green apple, sliced
4-5 ice cubes
orange/apple juice to smooth it out

Directions

Put all the ingredients in blender including some juice. Blend. Add more juice if necessary.

Carrot Smoothie/Serves 1

3 fresh carrots (peeled & chopped)
Cucumber (chopped approx 4 x 1 inch slices)
1 Golden Delicious apple (quartered & core removed)
2 handfuls cashew nuts
1/2 handful sunflower seeds
1 small cup fruit juice
3 tbsps fat-free yoghurt

Directions

Place all of the ingredients in the blender and blend until smooth.

Carrot & Tomato Smoothie/Serves 2

4 medium sized carrots, cut into 1 inch cubes
6 medium sized tomatoes, quartered
1 stalk celery, chopped into 1/2 inch pieces
1 tsp black pepper (freshly grounded)
2 tbsps fresh lemon juice

Directions

Blend all ingredients together, adding additional liquid to taste if necessary. Pour over crushed ice cubes.

Celery Smoothie/Serves 1

110ml/1/2 cup carrot juice
1 lb/450g tomatoes, skinned, seeded and roughly chopped
1 tbsp lemon juice
4 celery stalks, trimmed and sliced
4 scallions, trimmed and roughly chopped
30g/1/2 cup roughly chopped fresh parsley
1 well-packed cup fresh mint

Directions

Put the carrot juice, tomatoes, and lemon juice into a blender and blend gently until combined. Add the sliced celery along with the scallions, parsley, and mint and blend until smooth.

Apple & Avocado/Serves 2

1 apple
1/2 ripe avocado
1/2 apple juice
3 ice cubes
3 sprigs mint leaves
1 tsp freshly squeezed lime juice

Directions

Core and cut the apple into 4 pieces then combine all the ingredients together in a blender.

.

Broccoli Smoothie/Serves 1

2 cups of cut raw broccoli
1/2 cup of cut raw green cabbage
1 stick cut raw celery
1 cut peeled, de-cored apple or 3/4 cup apple juice

Directions

Blend all ingredients together until smooth. Add additional liquid (water) to taste.

Tomato Lemon Twist/Serves 1

2 tomatoes, cut in chunks
1 cup tomato juice (or 2-3 medium tomatoes, juiced)
1/2 lemon, juiced
1 tsp freshly grated lemon rind
6 fresh basil leaves, rinsed

Directions

Blend all ingredients on high speed and serve over crushed ice. Add black pepper to taste.

The recipes contained in this book are passed on in good faith but the publisher cannot be held responsible for any adverse results. Please be aware that certain recipes may contain nuts. The recipes use both metric and imperial measurements, and the reader should not mix metric and imperial measurements. Spoon measurements are level, teaspoons are assumed to be 5ml, tablespoons 15ml. For other measurements, see chart below. Times given are for guidance only, as preparation techniques may vary and can lead to different cooking times.

Spoons to millilitres

1/2 teaspoon	2.5 ml	1 Tablespoon	15 ml
1 teaspoon	5 ml	2 Tablespoons	30 ml
1-1 1/2 teaspoons	7.5 ml	3 Tablespoons	45 ml
2 teaspoons	10 ml	4 Tablespoons	60 ml

Grams to ounces

10g	0.25oz	225g	8oz
15g	0.38oz	250g	9oz
25g	1oz	275g	10oz
50g	2oz	300g	11oz
75g	3oz	350g	12oz
110g	4oz	375g	13oz
150g	5oz	400g	14oz
175g	6oz	425g	15oz
200g	7oz	350g	16oz

Metric to cups

Description		1 cup
Flour etc	115g	1 cup
Clear honey etc	350g	1 cup
Liquids etc	225ml	1 cup

Liquid measures

5fl oz	1/4 pint	150 ml
7.5fl oz		215 ml
10fl oz	1/2 pint	275 ml
15fl oz		425 ml
20fl oz	1 pint	570 ml
35fl oz		1 litre

This edition first published in 2009 by ImPulse Paperbacks, an imprint of Iron Press Ltd. © Iron Press Ltd 2009 Printed in China